FRANCIS FRITH'S

SWANAGE AND PURBECK

PHOTOGRAPHIC MEMORIES

RODNEY LEGG has emerged as Dorset's premier historian of the 20th century. He was born in Bournemouth in 1947 and founded both Tyneham Action Group and 'Dorset County Magazine' in 1968. 'Dorset Life' is the successor magazine. 'Purbeck Island', published in 1972, was his first full-sized book. He has since produced a further 90 titles, with frequent returns to his favourite landscapes in the Isle of Purbeck. Archaeology, military matters and the novelist Thomas Hardy are his chosen special subjects.

Current titles include 'Dorset's War Diary', 'Dorset's Hardy County' and 'Discover Stonehenge and Avebury'. As well as achieving public access to the Lulworth Ranges and persuading the National Trust to open Fort Henry at Studland, he has also registered large areas of open country in Purbeck under new legislation. Since 1989 he has been chairman of the Open Spaces Society and a member of the ruling council of the National Trust.

FRANCIS FRITH'S
PHOTOGRAPHIC MEMORIES

SWANAGE AND PURBECK

PHOTOGRAPHIC MEMORIES

RODNEY LEGG

First published in the United Kingdom in 2004 by
Frith Book Company Ltd

Limited Hardback Subscribers Edition Published in 2004
ISBN 1-85937-841-2

Paperback Edition 2004
ISBN 1-85937-842-0

British Library Cataloguing in Publication Data

Francis Frith's Swanage and Purbeck - Photographic Memories
Rodney Legg

Frith Book Company Ltd
Frith's Barn, Teffont,
Salisbury, Wiltshire SP3 5QP
Tel: +44 (0) 1722 716 376
Email: info@francisfrith.co.uk
www.francisfrith.co.uk

Printed and bound in Great Britain

The following images were supplied by Rodney Legg: T362001 (page 44)
T362002 (page 44)
W647002 (page 45)

Front Cover: **SWANAGE**, *The Promenade 1925* 78791
Frontispiece: **SWANAGE**, *From the Pier 1897* 40301

*The colour-tinting is for illustrative purposes only, and is not intended to
be historically accurate*

CONTENTS

FRANCIS FRITH
VICTORIAN PIONEER

FRANCIS FRITH, founder of the world-famous photographic archive, was a complex and multi-talented man. A devout Quaker and a highly successful Victorian businessman, he was philosophical by nature and pioneering in outlook.

By 1855 he had already established a wholesale grocery business in Liverpool, and sold it for the astonishing sum of £200,000, which is the equivalent today of over £15,000,000. Now a very rich man, he was able to indulge his passion for travel. As a child he had pored over travel books written by early explorers, and his fancy and imagination had been stirred by family holidays to the sublime mountain regions of Wales and Scotland. 'What lands of spirit-stirring and enriching scenes and places!' he had written. He was to return to these scenes of grandeur in later years to 'recapture the thousands of vivid and tender memories', but with a different purpose. Now in his thirties, and captivated by the new science of photography, Frith set out on a series of pioneering journeys up the Nile and to the

Near East that occupied him from 1856 until 1860.

INTRIGUE AND EXPLORATION

These far-flung journeys were packed with intrigue and adventure. In his life story, written when he was sixty-three, Frith tells of being held captive by bandits, and of fighting 'an awful midnight battle to the very point of surrender with a deadly pack of hungry, wild dogs'. Wearing flowing Arab costume, Frith arrived at Akaba by camel sixty years before Lawrence of Arabia, where he encountered 'desert princes and rival sheikhs, blazing with jewel-hilted swords'.

He was the first photographer to venture beyond the sixth cataract of the Nile. Africa was still the mysterious 'Dark Continent', and Stanley and Livingstone's historic meeting was a decade into the future. The conditions for picture taking confound belief. He laboured for hours in his wicker dark-room in the sweltering heat of the desert, while the volatile chemicals fizzed dangerously in their trays. Back in London he exhibited his photographs and was 'rapturously cheered' by members of the Royal Society. His reputation as a photographer was made overnight.

VENTURE OF A LIFE-TIME

Characteristically, Frith quickly spotted the opportunity to create a new business as a specialist publisher of photographs. He lived in an era of immense and sometimes violent change.

For the poor in the early part of Victoria's reign work was exhausting and the hours long, and people had precious little free time to enjoy themselves. Most had no transport other than a cart or gig at their disposal, and rarely travelled far beyond the boundaries of their own town or village. However, by the 1870s the railways had threaded their way across the country, and Bank Holidays and half-day Saturdays had been made obligatory by Act of Parliament. All of a sudden the working man and his family were able to enjoy days out and see a little more of the world.

With typical business acumen, Francis Frith foresaw that these new tourists would enjoy having souvenirs to commemorate their days out. In 1860 he married Mary Ann Rosling and set out on a new career: his aim was to photograph every city, town and village in Britain. For the next thirty years he travelled the country by train and by pony and trap, producing fine photographs of seaside resorts and beauty spots that were keenly bought by millions of Victorians. These prints were painstakingly pasted into family albums and pored over during the dark nights of winter, rekindling precious memories of summer excursions.

THE RISE OF FRITH & CO

Frith's studio was soon supplying retail shops all over the country. To meet the demand he gathered about him a small team of photographers, and published the work of independent artist-photographers of the calibre of Roger Fenton and Francis Bedford. In order to gain some understanding of the scale of Frith's business one only has to look at the catalogue issued by Frith & Co in 1886: it runs to some 670 pages, listing not only many thousands of views of the British Isles but also many photographs of most European countries, and China, Japan, the USA and Canada - note the sample page shown on page 9 from the hand-written Frith & Co ledgers recording the pictures. By 1890 Frith had created the greatest specialist photographic publishing company in the world, with over 2,000 sales outlets - more than the combined number that Boots and WH Smith have today! The picture on the next page shows the Frith & Co display board at Ingleton in the Yorkshire Dales (left of window). Beautifully constructed with a mahogany frame and gilt inserts, it could display up to a dozen local scenes.

POSTCARD BONANZA

The ever-popular holiday postcard we know today took many years to develop. In 1870 the Post Office issued the first plain cards, with a pre-printed stamp on one face. In 1894 they allowed other publishers' cards to be sent through the mail with an attached adhesive halfpenny stamp. Demand grew rapidly, and in 1895 a new size of postcard was permitted called the court card, but there was little room for illustration. In 1899, a year after Frith's death, a new card measuring 5.5 x 3.5 inches became the standard format, but it was not until 1902 that the divided back came into being, so that the address and message could be on one face and a full-size illustration on the other. Frith & Co were in the vanguard of postcard development: Frith's sons Eustace and Cyril continued their father's monumental task, expanding the number of views offered to the public and recording more and more places in Britain, as the

St Catherine's College
Senate House & Library
Gerrard Hostel Bridge
Geological Museum
Addenbrooke's Hospital
St Mary's Church
Fitzwilliam Museum, Pitt Press &c
Buxton, The Crescent
The Colonnade
Public Gardens
Haddon Hall, View from the Terrace
Millers Dale

coasts and countryside were opened up to mass travel.

Francis Frith had died in 1898 at his villa in Cannes, his great project still growing. The archive he created continued in business for another seventy years. By 1970 it contained over a third of a million pictures showing 7,000 British towns and villages.

FRANCIS FRITH'S LEGACY

Frith's legacy to us today is of immense significance and value, for the magnificent archive of evocative photographs he created provides a unique record of change in the cities, towns and villages throughout Britain over a century and more. Frith and his fellow studio photographers revisited locations many times down the years to update their views, compiling for us an enthralling and colourful pageant of British life and character.

We are fortunate that Frith was dedicated to recording the minutiae of everyday life. For it is this sheer wealth of visual data, the painstaking chronicle of changes in dress, transport, street layouts, buildings, housing, engineering and landscape that captivates us so much today. His remarkable images offer us a powerful link with the past and with the lives of our ancestors.

THE VALUE OF THE ARCHIVE TODAY

Computers have now made it possible for Frith's many thousands of images to be accessed almost instantly. Frith's images are increasingly used as visual resources, by social historians, by researchers into genealogy and ancestry, by architects and town planners, and by teachers involved in local history projects.

In addition, the archive offers every one of us an opportunity to examine the places where we and our families have lived and worked down the years. Highly successful in Frith's own era, the archive is now, a century and more on, entering a new phase of popularity. Historians consider the Francis Frith Collection to be of prime national importance. It is the only archive of its kind remaining in private ownership. Francis Frith's archive is now housed in an historic timber barn in the beautiful village of Teffont in Wiltshire. Its founder would not recognize the archive office as it is today. In place of the many thousands of dusty boxes containing glass plate negatives and an all-pervading odour of photographic chemicals, there are now ranks of computer screens. He would be amazed to watch his images travelling round the world at unimaginable speeds through internet lines.

The archive's future is both bright and exciting. Francis Frith, with his unshakeable belief in making photographs available to the greatest number of people, would undoubtedly approve of what is being done today with his lifetime's work. His photographs depicting our shared past are now bringing pleasure and enlightenment to millions around the world a century and more after his death.

SWANAGE AND PURBECK
AN INTRODUCTION

THE MAGICAL landscape of the Isle of Purbeck, the former royal hunting ground that forms the south-eastern arm of the Dorset coast, is celebrated in this selection of photographs which span a century. Purists who share my excitement in crossing the Wareham Causeway or arriving by ferry from Sandbanks will notice that I have stretched the boundaries to include houses and hamlets in the present-day area of Purbeck District Council. Things were ever thus, blurred by artistic licence, because even Lulworth Cove and Woolbridge Manor are just beyond the historic bounds of the peninsula that provided medieval marble for cathedrals and effigies across the land.

Winning the accolade of World Heritage Site designation at the turn of the millennium links the cliffs and hinterland of a geological wonderland with the associated geology to the west. Our coastline ages as one travels west. Its exploration, appropriately for the holiday coast, begins here with Swanage which has made the transformation from stone port into tourist town. 'Sunny Swanage' I always call it, with justification, as I am writing this after hearing on the midnight weather report that 'Swanage in Dorset was the sunniest place in Britain yesterday, with 14 hours of unbroken sunshine'. It vies with Torquay and Jersey for the honour of hot spot of the English Channel.

My onward route is northwards to Studland and Poole Harbour before moving across the stone plateau to Lulworth. The photographic selection then proceeds inland, via Corfe Castle and Wareham, to the hinterland at Wool, Bovington and Bere Regis.

In all places Frith's photographers have come up trumps. I'll highlight a few personal favourites. Seawards of the grounds of the Royal Victoria Hotel at Swanage you can see the rails of a tramway which led to the old pier. Sections can still be seen embedded in the present promenade. Being even more of an anorak, helped by Ron Barnes who worked for the company that carried a famous name, I spotted the masts and wires of Marconi's experimental wireless transmitters at Sandbanks. The original plate shows the precious cables to perfection, but as I detailed their significance Colin Leach joked that 'the printers will be able to remove them digitally!'.

Another picture which excited me - and this does prove the sad life I lead - was the shot showing hundreds of cars on the edge of the cliffs at Lulworth Cove. That was where we parked when we arrived for post-war Sunday picnics in an old Jowett and then our Standard Eight, in what is now regarded as an anachronistic eyesore. Other shots show its replacement on the other side of the Coastguard Cottages, out of sight of both the sea and the top-class housing in Britwell Drive. For real nostalgia addicts there are the paddle steamers, loaded to the gunwales, as the high spot of the week when the world and his wife came across the sea from Weymouth.

One place that strikes me as inauspicious for a honeymoon is Woolbridge Manor during its brief reincarnation as a country house hotel. Its most famous guest, one of the best-known heroines in English literature, was Tess Durbeyfield from Thomas Hardy's greatest novel. She arrived as a bride and left with her worst nightmare. Fact and fiction also overlap at Bere Regis where real-life Turberville tombs and the family's stained-glass memorial window form a perfect medieval setting.

As a romantic ruin, one of the finest of its kind in Britain and Europe, Corfe Castle is second to none in scale and setting. It is very English in character as a glorious failure, having been reduced to ragged and rugged beauty by demolition teams at the end of the Civil War. A more recent shell, photographed by me when gutted by fire in 1968, East Burton Dairy appears here as its former self in a rustic idyll predating the building of nuclear reactors on Winfrith Heath. Its ford failed to survive the arrival of heavy water.

Beauty is in the eye of the beholder, and to me Fort Henry on Redend Point - beside the grounds of the Manor Hotel at Studland - is one of the best chunks of concrete in the land. Its bomb- and shell-proof observation slit hosted King George VI, Winston Churchill and Dwight D Eisenhower, among others, as they watched the crucial live-fire rehearsals for D-Day. For years I ran a one-man campaign that eventually succeeded in having it opened to the public.

Westwards, riding a wave of popular support, I produced my own set of picture postcards. They feature Tyneham village as a time capsule in the Lulworth Ranges which were vastly expanded during the Second World War, six days before Christmas in 1943, in order to train tank crews for the forthcoming Battle of Normandy.

SWANAGE, *From The Coastguard Station 1897* 40308

These are my contribution to the contemporary record of what has turned from dispossession and depopulation into a wildlife refuge behind the most spectacular and varied coastline in England. On a much wider scale, Frith's photographers also capture enduring scenes to which we yearn to return, as well as precious glimpses of that other world which we have lost.

Of the hundred images that I selected, about a fifth feature what is now National Trust land on or adjoining the former Bankes Estate, whose reign of half a millennium at Corfe Castle and Studland ended in 1981 when the last owner, Ralph Bankes, bequeathed his lands to the nation. The adjuncts add to the romance and history, as they include Dorset's fantasy island in Poole Harbour - Brownsea had a succession of eccentric owners - and Dancing Ledge at Langton Matravers where it is 'the sea himself' who plays on a rocky shelf, as local quarrymen put it to local author Nina Warner Hooke.

Completion of the conservation of that corner of Purbeck, and containment of Swanage town, has been achieved by the creation of Durlston Country Park. This also brings public access to Anvil Point, overlooking climbers, divers and dolphins, plus an eccentric babel of wise words carved in stone for Victorian entrepreneur George Burt. He embraced both old certainties (poems and scripture) and new knowledge (astronomy and statistics). The practicalities of public order were also addressed with injunctions against discharging firearms or throwing stones.

The next major estate comprises Encombe House and 1,000 acres of its Golden Bowl, with its two miles of coast including some of the best shoots in southern England, which was sold by the Scott family in the summer of 2002 for £15 million. Handled by FPD Savills, it was the third most expensive British property transaction of the year, when sold to the American financier Charles McVeigh III, chairman of Schroder Salomon Smith Barney.

Then we come to the military lands from Kimmeridge to Lulworth Cove, and inland across the Purbeck Hills and the heath to the scrubby woods beside the River Frome. Northwards, also on the heath, is another great wedge of tank training country around the Royal Armoured Corps headquarters at Bovington. Adjoining the Ministry of Defence lands towards the coast, and renting the Government some of its 10,000 acres including Lulworth Camp, comes the Weld Estate. A similar symbiotic relationship exists to the north with the Frampton Estate at Moreton having spawned Bovington Camp. Postwar conifer plantations, notably Wareham Forest in the north and Rempstone Forest on the Ryder family's lands fringing Poole Harbour, provide the Forestry Commission's backdrop to the view from the Purbeck Hills. Many of the brown bits, representing some of the best lowland heath in Britain, are managed as national nature reserves.

Feudal Purbeck is still alive and well. It is fudged at the edges by institutional successors, such as the Defence Lands Agency, English Nature, the National Trust and the Royal Society for the Protection of Birds, but the joins in the landscape are almost seamless.

Beyond Poole Harbour, where market forces have created some of the most expensive urban living space this side of Tokyo, rampant suburbia rules for as far as the eye can see. Shades of blue at Sandbanks soon turn to grey. You don't have to be a John Betjeman to appreciate the difference.

SWANAGE

SWANAGE, *The Globe 1892* 31357

Newly-built Durlston Castle (top left) and the 40-ton Great Globe, also dating from 1887, are seen here from the south-east. The 'Sahara Desert' and 'Soudan' are writ large with 'Arabia' across the Red Sea. George Burt's three-dimensional educational extravaganza goes on to enlighten visitors with cosmic sizes and distances, scriptural and poetical quotations, and the fact that they are standing 'Above sea 136 feet'.

▼ **SWANAGE,** *From Durlston Castle 1892* 31354

Former 'quarr houses' and stone workings (bottom left) can be seen here beside Durlston Bay (lower right) which revealed fossils of the first marsupial-type mammals that succeeded the dinosaurs. Peveril Point and its strata of Purbeck marble jut out seawards (centre right) with the chalk cliffs of Ballard Point (top right) rising northwards across Swanage Bay. The cliff path, landscaped between stone walls, became Isle of Wight Road.

▶ **SWANAGE**
Tilly Whim Caves 1899
43774

This view is south-westwards from the quarry gallery to Anvil Point (centre left) where Purbeck's coast becomes a vertical wall of stone. Above (centre) is the lamp of Anvil Point Lighthouse, completed in 1882, after a series of shipwrecks which culminated with 77 being drowned here on the 1,230-ton sailing ship 'Alexandrovna' on 29 April that year.

◄ **SWANAGE**
*Tilly Whim Caves
c1950* S239023

Visitors stand in front of the galleries of the former Tilly Whim Quarry which was turned into a tourist attraction by Victorian contractor and developer George Burt in 1887. He chose an appropriate quotation from 'The Tempest' by William Shakespeare, to be inscribed on the rock face above:

'The cloud capped towers, the gorgeous palaces,

the solemn temples, the Great Globe itself.

Yea, all which it inherit, shall dissolve,

And like the baseless fabric of a vision

Leave not a rack behind.'

► **SWANAGE**
Tilly Whim Caves 1890
25551

This view shows the eastern gallery of the underground cliff quarry with one of George Burt's inscriptions (centre left) giving its potted history: 'These caves were formed centuries ago by men making sinks and rick-stones. Smuggling was also carried out here, and both were discontinued about the end of the French Wars, 1814.' To complete the impression of a dungeon, outside its gated entrance (centre right), Burt erected an octagonal column which he had removed from Pentonville Prison in London.

▶ **SWANAGE**
The Coastguard Station 1897 40310

This view shows Peveril Point, eastwards to its lookout and fort (far left), which with a semaphore mounted on Round Down, operated as a Royal Navy signal station during the Napoleonic Wars. After the peace with France, a Coastguard Station was built (centre), and the Lifeboat Station (centre right) was constructed for the 'Charlotte Mary' in 1875. She was replaced by two vessels that were both named 'William Erle' - the first proved unstable - in 1890 and 1893. Being the town's traditional defensive position, this was manned by weekend volunteers, with the mortars and cannon of No.7 Battery of the 2nd Volunteer Brigade, Southern Division of the Royal Artillery.

◀**SWANAGE**
From the Coastguard Station 1897
40308

This view is looking from Peveril Point to the Clock Tower (centre), showing its original spire, which was replaced by a cupola in 1904 after fundamentalist Christian protests that spires only belong on churches. Brought from London, it marked the north-eastern corner of contractor Thomas Docwra's Grove House estate. Peveril Tower (left), later renamed Rockleigh, dated from the early 1890s and was built by Edwin Williams. The 1859-built pier (centre foreground) operated in tandem with its 1895-built replacement (centre background), which is seen with a paddle steamer. The view is north-westwards to the skyline of Godlingston Hill (centre distance) and Ulwell Gap (top right).

▲ **SWANAGE,** *The Shore c1950* S239247

Rockleigh (top left) was demolished in 1986 and replaced by a Spanish-style marine village. The Clock Tower, clockless and with a cupola instead of its spire, was built as a memorial to the Duke of Wellington, on the Southwark side of London Bridge in 1854. It was demolished by Mowlem and Company in 1866 and shipped to Swanage by George Burt who presented it to fellow contractor Thomas Docwra who had just bought the Grove Estate. In the background of this view, westwards, are the two piers.

◄**SWANAGE**
The Pier 1894 34605

This view is from the Royal Victoria Hotel, formerly Swanage Manor, which was named for the overnight visit of Princess Victoria on 7-8 August 1833. The front lawn sloped south-eastwards to the timber pier (centre right) built by James Walton in 1859. A large sailing ship is berthed alongside. The princess and her mother, the Duchess of Kent, sailed across the bay from Norris Castle on the Isle of Wight, in the royal yacht 'Emerald', towed by a Royal Navy steamer. She left with a Swanage-made straw bonnet.

SWANAGE
The Pier 1897 40306

The view from the grounds of the Royal Victoria Hotel received its next addition in 1896 with the building of Alfred Thorne's second timber pier (centre). Unlike the first, which shared its planks with an industrial tramway, this was designed specifically for the burgeoning tourist trade. A new kiosk (centre right) opened for arrivals on foot.

SWANAGE, *From the Pier 1897* 40301

Victorians promenade on the newly-opened second Swanage pier. The townscape is in a state of transition, with Seymer Road (left) and the Royal Victoria Hotel (centre) representing the height of what was now being celebrated as 'the longest reign on record'. Stocks of quarry stone share the central shore with offices for the Wilts and Dorset Bank (centre), built by George Siley, though the bankers never moved into their new building. Tailor and yacht outfitter Edward Moffat and the Mowlem Institute (right) also occupied prime positions.

SWANAGE
The Pier from the Royal Victoria Hotel 1897 40307

This view shows the shoreline and an industrial tramway (centre) looking eastwards, to the two piers in Swanage Bay (top left). Some of the rails, which date from 1859, are still embedded in the promenade. A stone wall separates the working part of the seafront from the flower beds and lawns of the Royal Victoria Hotel. Beyond are Marine Villas (centre right) and the Clock Tower (centre). Princess Victoria, when she visited in 1833, arrived at the Stone Quay (centre left).

SWANAGE, *The Mill Pond 1890* 25548

The setting south-eastwards from the Mill Pond includes tenements in former Church Farm (left) and cottages on Church Hill (centre), though those below Wyvern Cottage have since been replaced by the present Rectory. Behind, with a great slab of walling to the rear of the High Street, is the extension to the Congregational Church dated 1837. Houses at Coniston Close (right) have also been rebuilt but the scene remains picturesque.

SWANAGE
Station Yard 1897
40303

The seaside end of the Isle of Purbeck branch railway arrived in Swanage from Wareham in 1885. Swanage Station and Station Road (centre right) can be seen beyond the Rectory (bottom right), the home of Rev Thomas Alfred Gurney, which is now Swanwic House. The view is north-eastwards from the tower of St Mary's Church to the double sidings of the goods yard (centre) and site of James Panton's Swanage Brewery which was demolished in 1893. Ballard Down (top left) and the Victorian villas of Gilbert Road (middle distance) form the backdrop.

21

▼ **SWANAGE,** *John Wesley's Cottage 1892* 31358

Wesley's Cottage, on the north side of the High Street to the west of the Town Hall, where the founding preacher of Methodism stayed on the night of 12-13 October 1774. It was damaged by a German bomb in an air raid on 14 May 1941, and demolished later in the Second World War. A commemorative plaque, visible on the ivy-clad gable end (centre left), has survived.

▶ **SWANAGE**
The High Street 1904 52886

Virginia Cottage is on the left, and the shop of shoemaker Fred Cox who was succeeded by Frank Cox. Behind is the Town Hall, built by Weymouth architect George Crickmay for George Burt in 1882, which incorporates the 1670-dated facade of Mercers' Hall. This stood in Cheapside and was the institute of London silk merchants. The gable end (top right) housed William Dixon's bakery. Next door, with an advertisement for the 'Dorset County Chronicle', is a traditional single-storey Purbeck cottage which became the Curiosity Shop from 1904 until 1914. It was demolished in 1959.

SWANAGE
Station Road 1925
78794

This photograph shows a policeman (centre) and one or two motor cars in a view westwards from the junction with Institute Road (bottom left). The National Provincial Bank and Trevose (left) are followed by the Domestic Bazaar, a bakery and the Post Office. Opposite are George Pond's Electric Cinema and the Grand Theatre with N D Rose's Central Garage adjoining. Buildings on the corner with Shore Road (right) include the unlikely combination of Tea Roof Gardens and Chocolate Shop and the premises of furnisher and undertaker Frank Smith.

SWANAGE
The Bay c1950 S239026

This view shows Shore Road and its taxi rank (left) with the beach shelter (centre) which was built in 1908; between it and the two K6 telephone kiosks (right) is John Mowlem's Column (centre right). This was built in 1862 and is topped by four Russian cannon balls from the Crimean War. These were hardly appropriate as trophies, because the column commemorates a supposed battle and victory against the Danes, offshore in 877. The chalk cliffs of Ballard Point - known locally as Ballard Head - form the backdrop.

▶ **SWANAGE**
The Promenade
c1955 S239254

A car emerges from Victoria Avenue on to Shore Road (lower right). The Walls ice-cream delivery van (bottom left) is beside beach kiosks and a 1910-built shelter, to which a clock was added in 1953, to commemorate the coronation of Queen Elizabeth II. Southwards, the far shore extends from the Hotel Grosvenor (centre left) and Royal Victoria Hotel (centre) to the Mowlem Institute (centre right).

◀ **SWANAGE**, *The Beach*
c1950 S239069

The people flocked back to the beach after wartime defences had been cleared. The Royal Engineers warned that dangers remained but town traders eagerly declared the town safe. The sappers were right, and a mine exploded beside crumbling cliffs near the Grand Hotel (centre), killing five schoolboys on Friday 13 May 1955. This view is northwards towards New Swanage, with Cliff Cottage and the Beach Restaurant and Stores (left centre) visible beyond the crowds.

▲ SWANAGE, *The Spa Cafe c1955* S239029

The beach is viewed from a groyne (bottom left) as the tide ebbs, in a view westwards across Shore Road (centre) to the Spa Cafe (centre). This cabin-like building below De Moulham Road advertises beach trays - on which teapots and cups were carried - and rental facilities on the sands include deck chairs and changing huts. These were the successors to White's bathing machines and Linnington's bathing tents.

◄ SWANAGE
The Beach c1955
S239025

A view of the sands and the town. The 19th-century skyline survived intact, westwards from the Hotel Grosvenor (top left) which overlooked Marine Villas and the twin piers. Peveril Downs are beyond and the Stone Quay and Royal Victoria Hotel next along the shore (centre). The Parade flats, at the back of Institute Road, extend to the 1863-built Mowlem Institute beside the junction with Shore Road (right).

SWANAGE
The Promenade 1925
78791

Linnington's Hygienic
Bathing Tents moved with
the times and now offered
'Mixed Bathing'. At the turn
of the century they were for
'Ladies Only' and protected
the privacy of users by
being pushed to the water
on wheels. John Davis White
then provided a 'Bathing
Saloon for Gentlemen'. The
view is northwards along
Shore Road to New Swanage
and the 1898-built Grand
Hotel (centre right).

◄ **SWANAGE**
*The Bay and
Highcliffe Steps c1960*
S239232

Steps from the Highcliffe (right) descend to the beach at North Swanage, beyond the promenade (upper centre) where the cliffs are skirted by beach huts. The 'Hut Office' of proprietor Harry Parsons offers deck chairs for hire. Ocean Bay Stores, with a flat roof and battlements (centre), was built as the Beach Restaurant for Frank Parsons by Bournemouth architect Thomas Grimes in 1908.

◄ **SWANAGE**
Ballard Head
1897 40312

There are overgrown sandpits above the junction of Victoria Road (centre left), and Beach Road (centre) which has since been re-named Shore Road. There was still an empty beach, apart from a few out-of-season bathing machines, between the town and its northern hamlet which begins with Cliff Cottage and Shore Cottage (upper left). Ballard Down (top) and Ballard Point (far right) - known locally as Ballard Head - provide the chalky backdrop.

▲ **SWANAGE,** *Highcliffe, Postcard Composite c1955* S239189

Highcliffe, which traded as Highcliffe Methodist Guild Guest House, first appeared as a name in 1902 and now applies to a cul-de-sac seawards from Ulwell Road. Extended eastwards, to absorb Mount Edgecombe villa, Highcliffe Hotel was run by Miss Hooke and Mrs Kelley. Thomas Shelston also offered apartments here in the Edwardian Monte Rosa.

◄ **SWANAGE,** *From Ballard Down 1899* 43767

The fields of Whitecliff Farm (foreground) hosted summer camps for militia and artillery volunteers in late Victorian times. New Swanage (centre right) is beginning to cluster around Ulwell Road and the 1898-built Grand Hotel (centre) at the northern end of the beach. The view is southwards across Swanage Bay to Peveril Point (centre left) and Peveril Downs (central skyline) on the other side of the town.

STUDLAND

SWANAGE, *Old Harry Rocks 1890* 25569

Chalk stacks off Handfast Point, the north-eastern extremity of the Purbeck Hills, display the dynamics of coastal erosion. Old Harry (right), as the Victorians knew him, was accompanied by a slender and though somewhat undercut Old Harry's Wife (left) until she was toppled in the 1890s by the gale that went on to sweep away the old chain pier at Brighton. Replacement partners are in the process of being formed. These Cretaceous rocks mark the eastern end of the Devon and Dorset World Heritage Site that is popularly known as the Jurassic Coast.

STUDLAND
On the Rocks c1955
S226009

Boulders of gritty reddish-brown heathstone below Redend Point (right), are typical of the Bagshot beds which underlie the Dorset heaths, in a view back in geological time to the uplifted chalk cliffs of Handfast Point and Old Harry Rocks (far centre). Almost all of Studland parish passed into National Trust ownership as part the bequest of landowner Ralph Bankes who died in 1981.

STUDLAND, *On the Beach c1950* S226002

Middle Beach (foreground) at Studland, is overlooked by the 1943-built Fort Henry on Redend Point (right-hand clifftop), which Canadian Engineers named for their home base in Ontario. The largest observation post in England, it was used by Allied generals who watched the live-firing rehearsals for the D-Day landings, and were joined by King George VI on 18 April 1944. Beside it is a gun emplacement (top right) dating from 1940 when the beach was defended against potential German invaders. Old Harry Rocks (far left) are to the south-east.

STUDLAND, *The New Inn 1890* 25557

The cottage on the east side of Manor Road (left) is the one to which Sergeant William Lawrence retired. He had moved across the leafy street from the New Inn, which in his time as landlord was known as the Duke of Wellington. Lawrence was one of Wellington's infantry, serving in the 40th Regiment of Foot in campaigns from South America and the Peninsular War - where he was wounded in the storming of Badajoz in 1812 - through to Waterloo in 1815, with eventual retirement in 1820.

STUDLAND, *Bankes Arms Hotel c1912* 43782

Partially rebuilt in 1910, the New Inn (centre right) was renamed the Bankes Arms Hotel, after the family that owned the parish. The cottage (left) of veteran soldier William Lawrence has since been demolished. The Bankes Arms, where the proprietor was Richard Clark, is now run by the Lightbown family.

POOLE HARBOUR

BROWNSEA ISLAND, *The Castle 1904* 52801

Marconi's yacht 'Electra' is moored in Brownsea Roads anchorage (centre left) with Branksea Castle beyond. Brownsea Island is an offshore 600 acres of Studland parish. Dating back to Henry VIII's coastal fort guarding the entrance to Poole harbour, Branksea Castle was gutted by fire on 26 January 1986, when owned by Kenneth Balfour MP. It was rebuilt as the home of wealthy socialites Charles and Florence van Raalte. Also facing eastwards are the 1842-dated Coastguard Station (centre), the Quay, and Quay Cottages (right).

BROWNSEA ISLAND
The Castle 1891 29623

An inland view of Branksea Castle (formerly Crichel House), looking eastwards from the island, showing the Gothic building erected after 1765 by Humphrey Sturt MP, as his country seat. Subsequent owners were Sir Charles Chad and Sir Augustus Foster, a retired diplomat, who slit his throat here in 1848. Colonel William Petrie Waugh extended the building (centre left) in 1853 but went bankrupt and fled to Spain in 1857.

SANDBANKS, *The Haven Hotel 1900* 46102

The remarkable features of this shot, north-eastwards from a timber jetty, actually stand between the buildings - the Haven Hotel (centre right), an 1898-built villa (left) in an acre of land that was bought by the Misses Cassidy from Ireland, and a Coastguard signal box (centre). Two of Guglielmo Marconi's experimental radio masts stand between the houses and there is either another radio mast or a flag-pole on the roof of the hotel. Wireless communication between England and France had been established by Marconi in 1899.

▶ **SANDBANKS**
Shore Road 1912 66148

Shore Road (left) and Banks Road (centre) lead from Poole and Lilliput to Sandbanks (far right). The waters of Poole Harbour are seen at high tide with the first incursions of Spartina cord grass which was an accidental introduction from Argentina.

◀ STUDLAND
The Ferry c1960 S226016

The lifeline between Poole and Purbeck, crossing between Sandbanks (right) and Shell Bay (left), is the Floating Bridge. 'Ferry No.1', dating back to the inauguration of the service in 1926, was supplemented by postwar 'Ferry No.2' in the 1920s. The first tended to break down and the second could only carry eight cars. In the picture is the much larger 'Ferry No.3' - they were otherwise unnamed - which was built by J Bolson and Son Limited of Poole. She came into service in 1958.

STONE COAST

SWANAGE
Anvil Point and the Lighthouse c1950 S239094

The Lighthouse was built by Trinity House on Anvil Point between 1880 and 1882, to fill the perilous gap between the rocks on Portland and the next cluster around the Isle of Wight. The imperative behind its building, below the earthworks of a former signal station on Round Down, was a series of shipwrecks which culminated with the loss of the 1,250-ton Liverpool sailing ship 'Alexandrovna' with her crew of 77, on Ragged Rocks below the western cliff (right).

LANGTON MATRAVERS
The Village c1960
L469015

Putlake Farm (centre), formerly part of the much larger Langton Manor Farm, was named for the puckish behaviour of the erratic Puck Lake stream. The view is westwards from the Ship Inn on Steps Hill to the village skyline around Durnford Drove (top left), the Hyde (upper centre) and the High Street (top right).

LANGTON MATRAVERS
The Quarry c1955
1469009

Derricks and quarries, past and present, dot the entirety of Langton Matravers parish from Castle View and the hamlet of Acton, across the plateau to South Barn and Blackers Hole. Underground workings, such as one preserved by the National Trust, represent the previous generation of mines. Much older, stretching from Langton West Woods, Wilkswood and Talbot's Wood to the Valley Road, are the bow-pits of mediaeval and Roman marble workings.

LANGTON MATRAVERS
St George's Church c1965 L469028

The squat 14th-century tower of the original mediaeval parish church (left) was dwarfed in 1875 by the huge nave (right) rebuilt by Weymouth architect George Crickmay. 'The edifice as it previously existed was long a grievous eyesore,' the 'Dorset County Chronicle' reported.

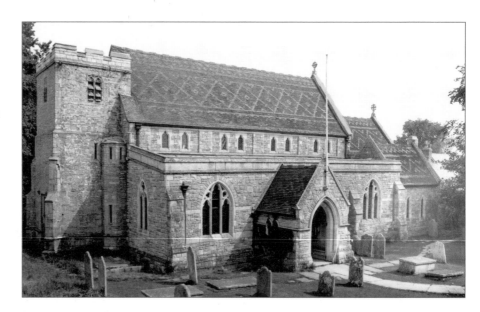

LANGTON MATRAVERS, *The King's Arms and High Street c1965* L469032

The King's Arms, at No.27 High Street (top left) was first licensed in 1742. Appropriately it was originally known as the Mason's Arms, and remains at the heart of Purbeck's stone-mining district. Prior's grocery shop, at No.31 (centre), became the Post Office Stores.

LANGTON MATRAVERS, *Dancing Ledge c1960* L469013

Originally quarried by the Hayward family and later rented to the Webber family, Dancing Ledge was owned by schoolmaster Thomas Pellatt of Durnford Preparatory School. He had the swimming pool cut into the rocks (lower centre left) so that his boys could still have their daily dip - stripped naked - when conditions were too rough for jumping into the sea. This spot features in the biography and private movies of avant-garde film director Derek Jarman. It was bought by the National Trust in 1992 and joined Trust land westwards to Seacombe (top left).

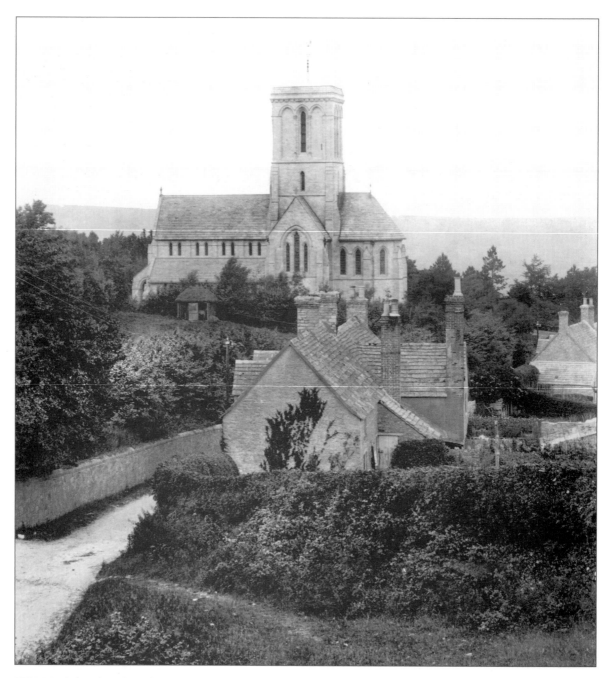

KINGSTON, *The Church 1899* 43788

St James' Church at Kingston, in effect the Scott family chapel of the Earls of Eldon from Encombe House, viewed looking southwards from cottages in South Street. It was built by London architect George Edmund Street (1824-91, between 1874 and 1880, on a scale that equated with a cathedral when compared with the original St James' Church on the other side of the estate-owned village.

WORTH MATRAVERS
St Nicholas' Church 1899 43791

The parish church of St Nicholas at Worth Matravers dates almost entirely from about 1100, though its fine Norman chancel arch was added in 1160. It seems to have been designed for an extension with a south chapel which was subsequently demolished. The view is from a public path a couple of walls away, south-eastwards to the roofs of Lobster Cottage and Stoneleigh (centre right).

ST ALBAN'S HEAD, *Bottom Valley 1899* 43789

Hill Bottom (centre), south-west of Renscombe Farm is seen here in a view towards Chapman's Pool and Houn's-tout Cliff The slopes of the Plain and St Alban's Head (left) rise to the south. Cottages in the deep gully in Hill Bottom housed a Victorian Coastguard Station, where Thomas Austin was the chief boatman in 1889, with six men as his crew.

▼ **TYNEHAM,** *The Village 1972* T362001

A concrete telephone kiosk and the Post Office (centre) stand behind military barbed wire at Tyneham. The public telephone has been identified by Michael Thomas as a K1 Mark 236 box of 1927, of which about 4,500 were erected, with a roof sign dating from 1929. Inside the building, the Post Office line was Kimmeridge 221. Mrs Gwendoline Driscoll was the shopkeeper when Tyneham was secretly evacuated on the orders of Churchill's War Cabinet, on Sunday 19 December 1943.

▶ **TYNEHAM**
The Rectory 1972 T362002

Gutted by fire in 1966, and since reduced to a single-storey shell, the Rectory in Tyneham village was built in 1853 for Rev Nathaniel Bond of Creech Grange. The last rector of Tyneham was Rev Humphrey Churchill Money, who was away serving with the Royal Engineers, when the Rectory was requisitioned by Southern Command, to extend the Lulworth Ranges, in 1943.

◀ **WORBARROW**
The Bay c1930
W647001

The fishing hamlet of Worbarrow (upper left), is seen here with Hill Cottage below Gold Down and Sea Cottage boathouses facing Worbarrow Bay. The view is south-eastwards from the slopes of Flower's Barrow hill fort, inside the area taken over for D-Day tank training on the Lulworth Ranges in 1943.

▶ **WORBARROW**
Sea Cottage 1972 W647002

Seen as a ruin, looking east from the beach of Worbarrow Bay, stone-roofed Sea Cottage was the home of generations of the Miller family. Fisherman Joe Miller lived there with cousin Jack Miller and the latter's wife, known as Miggie, when eviction notices were issued in 1943. This was one of a series of propaganda postcards, issued by the campaigning 1943 Committee and Tyneham Action Group which achieved the opening of weekend paths - the Lulworth Range Walks - in 1975.

LULWORTH

LULWORTH, *Durdle Door 1903* 49149

A steamer (centre) is framed by the rock arch of Durdle Door. This 'holed' opening (its Dorset dialect meaning) through hard Purbeck-Portland limestone juts offshore from the white cliffs between Man o' War Cove and a smaller hole in a promontory to the west at Bat's Head.

LULWORTH
The Cove 1925 78801A

This shows classic landform geology of what is now a gem of World Heritage status. Stair Hole (bottom right) and the contorted strata behind its breach in the seaward ridge show the forces generated by a collision of the Earth's tectonic plates. Eastwards is Lulworth Cove (centre), caused by the sea breaching through the Purbeck-Portland formations into softer Wealden sands and Cretaceous chalk in the dip beyond, in far more recent times.

49

LULWORTH, *Going Ashore c1955* L112023

'PS Victoria', operated by Cousens and Company from Weymouth, disembarks passengers. The view is south-eastwards to the eastern side of the entrance into Lulworth Cove. Paddle steamers sailed in and reversed out. Pepler's Point (top) is named for town planner Sir George Lionel Pepler (1882-1959) who rented Little Bindon as his holiday cottage for half a century.

LULWORTH
The Beach 1904
52716

The inner beach of Lulworth Cove and the boathouse (right), is shown looking southwards to the Coastguard Lookout (central skyline) from the cliffside stile on Bindon Hill (foreground). Rocks in the Cove (centre) still show a rectangular outline, which originated as a harbour and is also of historic interest as the site of oyster beds.

LULWORTH, *From the east, 1925* 78802

A paddle steamer is reversing out of Lulworth Cove, below the Coastguard Lookout (centre left). The view is south-westwards from Bindon Hill (right) down to the fishing boats on the beach between the boathouse and cafe, to Dungy Head (centre right).

LULWORTH
The Beach and a steam Boat c1955 L112043
Incredible numbers of people crammed aboard paddle steamers such as the 'Empress' (centre) which has just arrived in Lulworth Cove. They are about to walk the plank down to the shingle beach beside the cafe (bottom left). Lulworth was a favourite stopping point on services between Weymouth and Swanage. Within a decade scenes such as this had become a nostalgic memory.

▼ **LULWORTH,** *The Spring 1894* 34566

Water is emerging beside the aptly-named Spring Cottage which was built in about 1840, with fashionable French windows and a rustic veranda. Below is the Mill Pond, overlooked by Mill House Hotel and the range of Coastguard Cottages.

► **LULWORTH**
The Beach c1965
L112118

An inflatable landing is seen here typical of the new independent style of exploration popularised by the Zodiacs of television diver Jacques Cousteau. The view is south-westwards across to Little Bindon (middle right), where the original Bindon Abbey was founded.

◄ **LULWORTH**
The Car Park 1955
L112048
Cars used to park beside the Cove and are seen here in a view north-westwards from a mast stay (bottom left) to the Coastguard Cottages (centre), with Cove Hotel and Cromwell Hotel behind. Cove Cottage, Spring Cottage, and Mill House Hotel (centre right) looked out across 'the field with a thousand automobiles, which grows the best cash crop in Dorset'.

► **LULWORTH**
General View
c1965 L112096

Lulworth Cove and its hamlet (centre) are seen looking south-eastwards from Hambury Tout (left) to Bindon Hill, Swyre Head, and St Alban's Head (central horizon). The prominent villa beside Britwell Drive (centre right) is Oswald with Mary's Cottage, Weston and Tides being visible in the trees and scrub beyond.

◄ **LULWORTH**
The Village c1960
L112059

An inland view from Britwell Drive (foreground), looking northwards over the car park and a dozen coaches at the end of the B3070 in Lulworth Cove hamlet. West Lulworth village and Holy Trinity Church (centre) lie behind the sweep of Main Road. Prominent buildings include Bricklesey Cottage, the three-storey Cromwell Hotel, and a pair of thatched cottages.

◄ **WEST LULWORTH**
General View c1965 W543098

The village of West Lulworth is seen looking north-westwards from the slopes of Hambury Tout. Behind the buildings of Hambury Farm (foreground) are Church Road and Bindon Road (centre) with Main Road snaking through the picture. Holy Trinity Church is at the end of Church Road (left). Burngate Farm and Lulworth Camp are on the skyline (centre right).

▲ **EAST LULWORTH,** *St Andrew's Church 1894* 34599

Standing in the sylvan setting of Lulworth Park, the parish church of St Andrew's at East Lulworth has an impressive 15th-century tower that predates nearby Lulworth Castle. The remainder of the church was rebuilt in 1788, at the expense of Catholic landowner Thomas Weld, and again in 1864 by Dorchester architect John Hicks.

◄ **EAST LULWORTH**
An Old Cottage 1904
52721

Surviving 17th-century cottages (centre) stand opposite White Lodge Gate which is the main entrance into the grounds of Lulworth Castle. Almost all of the remainder of the original village was cleared and its community moved eastwards, for the creation of Lulworth Park between 1753 and 1785.

EAST LULWORTH
The Weld Arms Inn
1904 52720

The Weld Arms (left) is shown with the family's crest and motto 'Nil sine numine' above the second door (behind figure). The landlord's details were on a plaque in the recess above the first door: 'Edwin Bonham, Licensed to sell and retail Beer, Spirits and Tobacco to be consumed on the premises.' The slate-roofed house behind the cottage (centre right) was the Vicarage, where Rev William Davy Filliter was in residence.

EAST LULWORTH
Fishponds 1904 52727

The Lake and its island are found (centre) beside Lake Hill Plantation, between Home Farm and Coombe Heath to the north of Lulworth Park. It was created in 1837 by Joseph Weld of Lulworth Castle in order to test models of his racing yachts - which won him a £3,000 prize - and a brig he designed for the Admiralty.

CORFE CASTLE

CORFE CASTLE, *East Street 1899* 43784

The Greyhound Hotel (centre) and Corfe Castle ruins are shown looking north-westwards from East Street. The Reading Room, run by James Riddle, is behind the churchyard wall (left). Opposite (centre right), behind projecting Tuscan columns matching the frontage of the Greyhound Hotel, is the 1881-installed blind and shop front of provisions dealer George Cleall. Next door is a datestone for 1781 at September Cottage. Merrilees, with dormers, is followed by No.33, also with an attic room.

▶ **CORFE CASTLE**
*From the Church
Tower 1897* 40318

The view was taken from the tower in the time of Rev Eldon Surtees Bankes, the rector since 1854. The newly erected cross for Queen Victoria's diamond jubilee (centre foreground) faces Refreshment Rooms (bottom left) and the shop front towards the centre carries the name of grocer Robert Thomas Chipp who had recently succeeded baker and seedsman John George Luker. The Greyhound Hotel (bottom right) was run by Miss Mary Desallioud. The view is northwards to the railway viaduct and Norden claypits (far right).

◀ **CORFE CASTLE**
The Cross 1899 43786

Villagers call it the Square but to historians this is the Market Place. King John gave it a weekly Saturday market in 1215 with Thursdays being added by Henry III in 1248. The Town Pump and Market Cross (centre) have ancient steps and a relatively recent shaft, erected to celebrate Queen Victoria's diamond jubilee in 1897. Beyond is the 18th-century Town House, with the Mayor's robing room upstairs, and teas offered downstairs at 8d each. Behind are the nave and tower of the parish church of St Edward the Martyr.

▲ **CORFE CASTLE** *1890* 25568

The ruins are seen from the village, above the Wicken Stream and Oliver Vye's Lane (bottom left). The 12th-century Keep (centre) towers over the late 11th-century Gloriette and the remains of the King's Hall from King John's time (top right). Curtain defences include the Butavant Tower (top left), South Tower, North Tower, South-west Gatehouse, Fourth Tower, Third Tower and Second Tower (centre right). The collapsed First Tower (foreground) was reduced to this state in March 1646 in punishment for having been on the Royalist losing side in the English Civil War.

◄ **CORFE CASTLE**
The Village 1890 25582

The South-west Gatehouse (left) stands on the site of the assassination of the 15-year-old Anglo-Saxon King Edward on the evening of 18 March 978. He is commemorated by the parish church of St Edward the Martyr (centre right). Oliver Vye's Lane (lower right) runs below the ruined mediaeval towers of the Outer Bailey.

CORFE CASTLE
East Street 1931 84891

The best of the timeless views is still unchanged here, though with the Reading Room (left) now having become the Box of Delights and providing visitors with ice cream. Cleall's Stores remains in business and a slightly wider camera angle brings in the steps of No.35 (far right).

WAREHAM

WAREHAM, *The River Frome c1960* W173110

Wareham is seen here from South Bridge, looking westwards to the banks of the Anglo-Saxon Town Walls and Castle Close (centre right), built by Edward Seymer Clark on the footings of a Norman fortress. Abbot's Quay is to the right.

WAREHAM
View on the River
1950 W173074

Cars are parked on the quay (left) in front of the Old Granary Tea Rooms and Gardens (centre left), established by Miss P M Carter and her friend Miss S L J I Sydenham in the former warehouse of Oakley Brothers corn merchants. The view is eastwards, downstream to Redcliffe Farm (centre left) and Ridge hamlet (right).

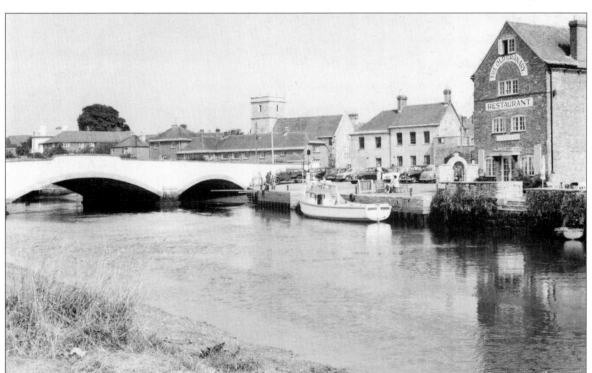

WAREHAM, *The River and Bridge c1965* W173112

This view looks north-westwards from the south bank to the 1927-built South Bridge (left) which replaced a graceful five-arch Norman bridge. Abbot's Quay and Holy Trinity Church (centre) are beyond. The other buildings are Bridge House and the Old Granary Restaurant (right).

► WAREHAM
St Mary's Church c1960
W173114

This view was taken looking over the River Frome towards the 15th-century tower and 1841-rebuilt nave of Lady St Mary parish church (centre top). The Priory (centre middle), a cell of Lire abbey in Normandy, dates from the early 12th century, with present buildings from the early 16th century.

The Church of St Martin
c1960 W173031

Wareham St Martin's (right), standing on King Alfred's Town Walls, is Dorset's earliest complete church. Anglo-Saxon arcading was replaced by Norman arches in the 12th century. The view is northwards from North Street, down to the sign of the former Lord Nelson public house (centre). The garage of Northover and Company, coach-builders, is at No.75 (left). Next door is early 19th-century No.77, and the trees screen Elm House which was Albert Edward Skewes's academy for boys.

WAREHAM
South Street c1960
W173117

This view looks northwards from No.16 (left), and shows the late 18th-century Black Bear Hotel, of three storeys with balustrade parapet. No.12 was Ernest Cox's family goods shop and No.10 housed Sansom and Co. ironmongers. Electrician Cyril Cottee traded from No.4. Opposite are Charles White's fried fish shop (right), in No.15, with butcher Levi Riggs next-door in No.17.

73

WAREHAM
North Street 1949
W173034

This view looks southwards from the National Provincial Bank (left) and the Red Lion Hotel (right). The Town Hall (top left) was rebuilt in 1870 with a Gothic clock tower and spire. In the distance are South Street and Bridge House (centre). The corner buildings (centre right) comprise No.2 South Street and No.1 West Street, with one of George Dicker's grocery stores being next door to confectioner Mrs Annie Jones.

WAREHAM, *West Street 1949* W173035

This view shows West Street looking eastwards from the office of borough surveyor Peter Byrne in No.12 (left) to Cleeve Brothers' garage in No.8. The Town Hall spire is at the crossroads (centre). The sign of the south side of the street was for George Dicker's butchers and grocery store.

INLAND

STOBOROUGH, *The Garage c1955* S447002x

Stoborough Garage (centre) was owned for many years by Gordon Hands, who was also the motor engineer at Holton Heath. Offering both Shell and British Petroleum, this was established beside what used to be the A351 road into the Isle of Purbeck. Wareham's South Causeway (centre right) is glimpsed between the thatched cottage and the coach. The building beside the latter is the King's Arms (right).

STOBOROUGH
The Village c1955
S447004

The Post Office (centre) on the east side of Corfe Road was run by the Head family for more than half a century. Ernest Alexander Head was the postmaster and his father, Horace Alfred Head, had been the village grocer and baker since before the First World War. Nutcrack Lane, leading to Arne, is the narrow turning between the houses.

STOBOROUGH, *The Caravan Site c1955* S447007

The postwar Lookout Caravan Park was sited on one of Harry Ridout's fields at Hyde Hill, beside Corfe Road. These days there are about 25 mobile homes in full-time occupancy. The notice on the gate cautions against backing out into the main road.

STOBOROUGH
Ridge Crossroads
c1955 S447009

Harphill Cottages (left) in the hamlet of Ridge, shown looking north-eastwards from New Road (foreground) into Barnhill Road (centre) which leads to Redcliffe Farm and its yacht club. Nutcrack Lane (left) is from Stoborough, and Arne is signed to the east (right). To the south, 172 acres of Sunnyside Farm were acquired by English Nature in 2001.

WAREHAM, *The Blue Pool c1955* W173018

The Blue Pool at Furzebrook, the best known of Purbeck's former heathland claypits was dug by Watts, Hatherley and Burns of Newton Abbot, in 1846. By 1953, after it had filled with water, T T Barnard of Furzebrook House had the bright idea of turning it into a beauty spot. Vivid and changing turquoise shades are caused by diffracted light passing through minute particles of clay in permanent suspension in the water. To the surprise of visitors, this blueness is at its strongest on an overcast day, when minimal sunlight is reflected off the surface.

▼ **BINDON ABBEY** *1894* 34616

Graves and ivy-clad ruins are shown beside the Monks' Cemetery of Bindon Abbey. The community was founded for the Cistercian Order by William de Glastonia in 1149. Its original establishment was on the eastern side of Lulworth Cove. Roger de Newburgh moved them here, inland to a mill and meadows beside the River Frome in 1172.

▶ **BINDON ABBEY**
The Gateway 1894
34614

The Gatehouse of the present Bindon Abbey, in the grounds of its mediaeval predecessor, was built by Thomas Weld between 1794 and 1798. A Gothic-style house, it incorporated a Catholic chapel on the first floor, and was in use for services from 1886 until the year before this photograph was taken.

◄ **WOOL**
The Stream in the Village Street
c1950 W344002

Stone and cob cottages and buildings stand beside the entrance to Sexeys Farm (left) in a view southwards to Wool Farm (centre) and Church Lane. Picturesque Spring Lane, to the east of the High Street, used to be the main road through the village.

► **WOOL**
A Thatched Cottage c1965
W344093

Seaforth Cottage, a neat and symmetrical Georgian Cottage ornée with rustic porch, would not look out of place on Marine Parade in Lyme Regis. It faces Spring Street from the junction with Church Lane. Behind (centre left) stands the tower of Holy Rood parish church.

WOOL
Woolbridge Manor Hotel and the River Frome c1965 W344097

This view shows cottages in the trees (top left), Wool Bridge (centre) and Woolbridge Manor (behind) during its period as a country house hotel. All the buildings, including the northern barns (top right), incorporate mediaeval stonework. The property belonged to Bindon Abbey until the dissolution of the religious houses in 1539, and was then granted to Sir Thomas Poynings, before the arrival of the Turberville family from Bere Regis.

► **WOOL**
The River c1955 W344030

Thatched cottages (right) stand between Woolbridge Manor and the River Frome, looking upstream from the five mediaeval arches of Wool Bridge. The river was bridged before 1343 and the present stonework dates from the 16th century.

◄ WOOL
Woolbridge Manor Hotel c1965 W344072

One of the earliest brick houses in Purbeck, rebuilt in 1660, Woolbridge Manor was the home of the Turberville family. Angel Clare brings his bride here for the pivotal twist in the tale of Thomas Hardy's 'Tess of the d'Urbervilles'. The reset circular panel above the north-facing front door dates from 1635 and carries the initials I S.

▶ **EAST BURTON**
The Water Splash
c1950 E267005

These days this idyllic scene seldom attracts a second glance. Its first loss was the stream from East Knighton, forded by Burton Road, which was put into a culvert. East Burton Dairy House (centre) was destroyed by fire in 1968. The view is north-eastwards, across East Burton Road, to Water Meadow Lane and Snipe Cottage (top right).

◀ **MORETON**
The Post Office
c1955 M308008

The Street is shown looking westwards from Wheelbarrow Cottage (left) and the K6-design telephone kiosk beside Moreton Post Office (right). The long range of 18th-century thatched cottages (centre) make this cul-de-sac a delightful time warp.

▲ **MORETON,** *The School c1955* M308005

The Church of England's National School (centre) was built in 1860 to provide for 120 pupils. It became an Elementary School and was taken over by Dorset County Council under the Education Act, 1901. The schoolhouse adjoins it (right). Since closed, the former schoolroom became Moreton Tea Rooms and Restaurant in 2001.

◀ **BOVINGTON**
The Woods, Menin Road c1955 B734001

Pine trees west of Bovington Camp, crossed by Menin Road which for the first generation of tank crews brought back memories of Passchendaele. Field Marshal Sir Douglas Haig had ordered the Second Army northwards into the Menin Road Sector on 16 August 1917 and after delays for preparations, plus bad weather, the great offensive began on 20 September 1917.

BERE REGIS
c1955 B480010

Bere Regis village is seen looking north-eastwards down the A35 (foreground and right) from the junction (left) with Doddings Lane, as Froom's Lane is locally known. Court Farm Cottage (centre left) stands beside the site of the former Manor House at Court Green. Other prominent buildings are the parish church (centre) and Royal Oak Inn (right of centre).

BERE REGIS, *General View c1960* B480029

Southbrook Farm is seen from Doddings Lane westwards to Rye Hill (centre left) and Black Hill (top left). The mature tree (left), a 200-year-old English elm, succumbed to fungal infection spread by bark beetles as Dutch Elm Disease ravaged the countryside in the early 1970s.

BERE REGIS, *The River, Southbrook c1960* B480016

The Bere Stream, seen looking eastwards from Southbrook Bridge, towards Bedford and Jesty's watercress beds with a glimpse of Woodbury Hill (top left). Pure water produced by artesian wells from the chalk aquifer, inspired the Silva Springs re-branding of the crop that came to fame for Victorian high tea in the Midlands and the North.

BERE REGIS, *The Church c1960* B480030

The parish church of St John the Baptist is shown from the north-east. One of the finest medieval churches in Dorset, with an outstanding decorated roof and Turberville family effigies, the tower (top) and Morton Chapel (centre) were added in the 16th century. The North Aisle (right of centre) was rebuilt in the 14th century.

INDEX

NAMES OF SUBSCRIBERS

The following people have kindly supported this book by subscribing to copies before publication

Samuel Aggas - aged 3, Swanage

The Alans, Corfe Castle

Shirley & John Albin, Swanage

D & E F J Anderson, Swanage

Keith & Donna Ashcroft, Swanage

Larry Ashton

L P & M R Bartlett, Bere Regis, Dorset

The Reverend W. Blakey, Rector of Wareham

In Memory of R Blandford, Purbeck

Bob Bonfield, Swanage

The Bonfield Family, Gully Coombe

Bill & Brenda Bradford, Swanage

Jim Bradford & Family, Langton Matravers

Jim & Sheila Brett

Don Brooks, Wareham

To my Dad, Stan Burgess, Wareham, Dorset

Laurence Cade, Photographer, London

To our sons Dani & Santos Calvo - Westcott

Bob Campbell, Swanage

E M A Cassidy

In Memory of Bob Chacksfield, Swanage

Memories of 'Charlies Band' Linnington, Swanage

Doris E Churchill, Studland

Royston C Churchill

Mr & Mrs Gordon Collins, Swanage

Mr & Mrs M Collins, Langton Matravers

Roderic Cooke, Swanage

Corfe Castle Library

Tony & Linda Coulson, Wool

To the Crabb Family in Sherborne

Dorchester Library

Philip & Pamela Dorey, Swanage

Mick & Shirley Dunlop, Swanage

Len & Juliet Eden, Churston Ferrers

Larry & Barbara Erickson, Chicago, USA

In Memory of Esther, Joe, Nadine & Clem

Nick, Melanie & Adam Field, Swanage

To Brian & Bridget Fudge, Henstridge

Kath & Cyril Gardener, Swanage

Jack & Joyce Gaynor, Swanage

Emily Alice Green, Sandford Woods

To my friend, Eileen Hardy, Swanage

In Memory of Alan Harris, Swanage

Brenda & Ken Harvey, Stonecourt, Swanage

David Haysom, Hon Curator Swanage Museum

David & Susan Head of Purbeck View, Swanage

To Christine Holland on her birthday

To Di Hooley in Queen Camel

David & Elizabeth Hunt, Swanage

Jeannie, Happy Christmas with my love
Anthony

In Memory of Jane Jolly, Hayes, Middx

Jean Jolly, Hayes, Middx

Martin Christopher Jones

To K & L Kellaway

Mr R Kellock, West Lulworth, Dorset

Mahesh-G Vaikom Kottaym, Kerala, S India

Marian & Mark Legall, Swanage

Alan & Lynda Macey, Wool, Dorset

Donald & Glenice Mack, Swanage

Frank & Teresa Martin, Wareham

Mrs M G Miller, Corfe Castle

The Mounsey Family, Langton Matravers

Dr C B A & Mrs C E Musselwhite,
Swanage

Mr Grayham Norman In Memory of Dad

To Brenda & Fred Pitfield, Bere Regis

To Di & Tony Poyntz-Wright

Stuart & Lorna Randall, Exeter

Mr Gerry Randle & Mrs Jean Randle

Geraldine Reid, Memories of my dear Bill

In Memory of Eva & Basil Richards

In Memory of Mrs L T Senior, Swanage

In Memory of George Henry Smith,
Wareham

Gerry & Sylvia Smith, Swanage

John P C Smith

Thomas A F Smith

Vivien June & John William Smith

Karel & Lynda Smits, Corfe Castle

Col (Retd) D S Squirrell & Mrs D S
Squirrell

To Steve & Lynn love Dad & Edna

In Memory of Nell & Harry Stockley

Swanage Library

Mr & Mrs Tait, Swanage

Harry Tatchell, Langton Matravers

P A Townson

Annemarie Van De Pasch, Swanage

Mike, Zoe & Hannah Varney, Swanage

Enid & Peter Verge

Dave & Darri Ward, Corfe Castle

Wareham Library

E A A & M Warne, Wareham

Haydn & Nicky Welch, Churchinford

Mark & Liz Welch, Taunton

The Western Family, Corfe Castle

Serena & Christian Westwood

Kenneth Wharton, Swanage

In Memory of T Lemon
Wheelwright, Swanage

Carlo M Wiggins, Swanage

The Wiggins Family, Swanage

Mr Paul Wilson, Mr Douglas Wilson

Mark & Sally Woolley, Swanage

Peter D Wright, Swanage

FRITH PRODUCTS & SERVICES

Francis Frith would doubtless be pleased to know that the pioneering publishing venture he started in 1860 still continues today. Over a hundred and forty years later, The Francis Frith Collection continues in the same innovative tradition and is now one of the foremost publishers of vintage photographs in the world. Some of the current activities include:

Interior Decoration

Today Frith's photographs can be seen framed and as giant wall murals in thousands of pubs, restaurants, hotels, banks, retail stores and other public buildings throughout the country. In every case they enhance the unique local atmosphere of the places they depict and provide reminders of gentler days in an increasingly busy and frenetic world.

Product Promotions

Frith products are used by many major companies to promote the sales of their own products or to reinforce their own history and heritage. Frith promotions have been used by Hovis bread, Courage beers, Scots Porage Oats, Colman's mustard, Cadbury's foods, Mellow Birds coffee, Dunhill pipe tobacco, Guinness, and Bulmer's Cider.

Genealogy and Family History

As the interest in family history and roots grows world-wide, more and more people are turning to Frith's photographs of Great Britain for images of the towns, villages and streets where their ancestors lived; and, of course, photographs of the churches and chapels where their ancestors were christened, married and buried are an essential part of every genealogy tree and family album.

Frith Products

All Frith photographs are available Framed or just as Mounted Prints and Posters (size 23 x 16 inches). These may be ordered from the address below. From time to time other products - Address Books, Calendars, Table Mats, etc - are available.

The Internet

Already fifty thousand Frith photographs can be viewed and purchased on the internet through the Frith websites and a myriad of partner sites.

For more detailed information on Frith companies and products, look at these sites:

www.francisfrith.co.uk
www.francisfrith.com
(for North American visitors)

See the complete list of Frith Books at:

www.francisfrith.co.uk

This web site is regularly updated with the latest list of publications from the Frith Book Company. If you wish to buy books relating to another part of the country that your local bookshop does not stock, you may purchase on-line.

For further information, trade, or author enquiries please contact us at the address below:
The Francis Frith Collection, Frith's Barn, Teffont, Salisbury, Wiltshire, England SP3 5QP.
Tel: +44 (0)1722 716 376 Fax: +44 (0)1722 716 881 Email: sales@francisfrith.co.uk

---

See Frith books on the internet at www.francisfrith.co.uk

FREE MOUNTED PRINT

Mounted Print
Overall size 14 x 11 inches

Fill in and cut out this voucher and return
it with your remittance for £2.25 (to cover postage and handling). Offer valid for delivery to UK addresses only.

Choose any photograph included in this book.
Your SEPIA print will be A4 in size. It will be mounted in a cream mount with a burgundy rule line (overall size 14 x 11 inches).

**Order additional Mounted Prints
at HALF PRICE (only £7.49 each*)**
If you would like to order more Frith prints from this book, possibly as gifts for friends and family, you can buy them at half price (with no additional postage and handling costs).

Have your Mounted Prints framed
For an extra £14.95 per print* you can have your mounted print(s) framed in an elegant polished wood and gilt moulding, overall size 16 x 13 inches (no additional postage and handling required).

---

* IMPORTANT!

These special prices are only available if you order at the same time as you order your free mounted print. You must use the ORIGINAL VOUCHER on this page (no copies permitted). We can only despatch to one address.

Send completed Voucher form to:
The Francis Frith Collection, Frith's Barn, Teffont, Salisbury, Wiltshire SP3 5QP

CHOOSE ANY IMAGE FROM THIS BOOK

Voucher for *FREE* and Reduced Price Frith Prints

Please do not photocopy this voucher. Only the original is valid, so please fill it in, cut it out and return it to us with your order.

Picture ref no	Page no	Qty	Mounted @ £7.49	Framed + £14.95	Total Cost
		1	Free of charge*	£	£
			£7.49	£	£
			£7.49	£	£
			£7.49	£	£
			£7.49	£	£
			£7.49	£	£
Please allow 28 days for delivery			* Post & handling (UK)		£2.25
			Total Order Cost		£

Title of this book . . . .

I enclose a cheque/postal order for £ . . . .
made payable to 'The Francis Frith Collection'

OR please debit my Mastercard / Visa / Switch / Amex card
(credit cards please on all overseas orders), details below

Card Number

Issue No (Switch only)   Valid from (Amex/Switch)

Expires   Signature

Name Mr/Mrs/Ms ....

Address ....

....

....

.... Postcode ....

Daytime Tel No ....

Email ....

Valid to 31/12/05

Free Print – see overleaf

Would you like to find out more about Francis Frith?

We have recently recruited some entertaining speakers who are happy to visit local groups, clubs and societies to give an illustrated talk documenting Frith's travels and photographs. If you are a member of such a group and are interested in hosting a presentation, we would love to hear from you.

Our speakers bring with them a small selection of our local town and county books, together with sample prints. They are happy to take orders. A small proportion of the order value is donated to the group who have hosted the presentation. The talks are therefore an excellent way of fundraising for small groups and societies.

Can you help us with information about any of the Frith photographs in this book?

We are gradually compiling an historical record for each of the photographs in the Frith archive. It is always fascinating to find out the names of the people shown in the pictures, as well as insights into the shops, buildings and other features depicted.

If you recognize anyone in the photographs in this book, or if you have information not already included in the author's caption, do let us know. We would love to hear from you, and will try to publish it in future books or articles.

Our production team

Frith books are produced by a small dedicated team at offices in the converted Grade II listed 18th-century barn at Teffont near Salisbury, illustrated above. Most have worked with the Frith Collection for many years. All have in common one quality: they have a passion for the Frith Collection. The team is constantly expanding, but currently includes:

Paul Baron, Jason Buck, John Buck, Ruth Butler, Heather Crisp, David Davies, Isobel Hall, Julian Hight, Peter Horne, James Kinnear, Karen Kinnear, Tina Leary, Stuart Login, David Marsh, Sue Molloy, Glenda Morgan, Wayne Morgan, Kate Rotondetto, Dean Scource, Eliza Sackett, Terence Sackett, Sandra Sampson, Adrian Sanders, Sandra Sanger, Julia Skinner, Lewis Taylor, Shelley Tolcher, Lorraine Tuck and Jeremy Walker.